NO AR

S0-AEE-019

DRUGS AND STRESS

Everyday routines and schedules create a certain amount of stress.

DRUGS AND STRESS

M.W. Buckalew, Jr.

THE ROSEN PUBLISHING GROUP, INC.
NEW YORK

For Erin and Adam

The people pictured in this book are only models. They in no way practice or endorse the activities illustrated. Captions serve only to explain the subjects of photographs and do not in any way imply a connection between the real-life models and the staged situations.

Published in 1993, 1998 by the Rosen Publishing Group, Inc.
29 East 21st Street, New York, NY 10010

Revised 1998

Copyright © 1993, 1998 by the Rosen Publishing Group, Inc.

Library of Congress Cataloging-in-Publication Data

Buckalew, M. W.
  Drugs and stress / M. W. Buckalew, Jr.
      p.   cm. — (The Drug abuse prevention library)
  Includes bibliographical references and index.
  Summary: Discusses the danger of specific drugs, explains how
    taking drugs to relieve tension or stress is likely to reinforce the
    problems and create greater stress, and suggests healthy ways to
    handle stress.
  ISBN 0-8239-2617-6
  1. Drug Abuse. 2. Teenagers—Drug use. 3. Stress in adolescence.
  [Drug abuse.] I. Title. II. Series.
  HV5809.5B83 1993
  362.29'0835—dc20   93-20288
                                                          CIP
                                                           AC

Manufactured in the United States of America

Contents

Introduction

*A*lthough there isn't a class for it, one of the things you're supposed to learn in high school is to learn to be yourself. The reason there isn't a class for it is because it can't really be taught in a classroom setting. Instead, it's just assumed that because you're getting older, you're becoming who you want to be. But that isn't always the case.

For some people, being a high school student is the hardest time of their lives. They get teased by other kids. If they don't learn as fast as other students, teachers give them a hard time. Their parents yell at them if they get bad grades or don't keep up with household chores. Coaches and gym teachers leave them out of games because they're not skilled enough. When any of these things happen, it can cause stress.

Stress can mean being worried or scared. It can mean being angry, or unhappy, or all these things. But stress is hard to take care of because you can't see it. When you accidentally cut your hand, you put a bandage on it, and the cut heals. How do you heal something you can't see?

Some people try to heal stress by using drugs. They think that because the drugs make them feel high, the problems that cause their stress will go away. But the problems don't go away. In fact, they get bigger. It would be like making a cut deeper instead of putting a bandage on it.

Most Americans are "on drugs" right now. Most people are having, or have just had, a cup of coffee, a soda, a cigarette, or an alcoholic drink. All these contain drugs. While these are legal, unlike marijuana, cocaine, or heroin, some teens don't know when they've crossed the line into abuse.

This book is about making your life enjoyable. One way to do that is to recognize the causes of stress and find solutions to deal with it. People have stress everyday, at any time. And people deal with it in different ways. It's important to learn to handle stress without drugs.

Stress may be the result of built-up pressures and worries.

CHAPTER 1

What Is Stress?

*T*here's an old story that, if told today, might go something like this:

A young student named David went in to tell his teacher, Mr. Garcia, that he didn't do his assignment.

"I couldn't," David said. "I was too stressed out."

"What's this?" Mr. Garcia gasped. "You were too stressed out? I'm so sorry to hear that. What's wrong? Are some of the other kids picking on you?"

"No," David answered, "nobody's picking on me."

"Is there trouble at home?" Mr. Garcia asked.

10 "No," David said, "no trouble at home."

"I see," the teacher said. "Do you feel the class is going too fast? Are you having a hard time keeping up with the other students?"

"No," said David, "I can keep up."

"Hmmm . . . do you feel the due date was unfair? Did I not give you enough time to finish the assignment?"

"No," answered David, "I had enough time."

"Well David, I don't understand," the teacher explained. "No one's picking on you, there's no trouble at home, you're keeping up with your studies, and you've had enough time to do the work. What is it that's stressing you out?"

David looked at the floor and then up at Mr. Garcia.

"Gee . . . I don't know."

Identifying Stress

David's story shows the problem. While David felt stressed out, he couldn't identify the causes of his stress. You cannot avoid stress because it comes from inside yourself. Think about facing the tough guys in the hall. Think about trying to write a paper for English class.

Think about not having enough money to buy something you really want.

All those things are called *stressors*. And the way you react to them is stress. When you worry about something, your body changes in an effort to cope with the problem.

Your body makes hormones, chemicals that flow through your blood and change the way you feel. They make you feel tense and uptight. They make butterflies in your stomach. Your heart may pound, your voice may become shaky, and your hands may feel cold. And all that makes it hard to think clearly.

The hormones are getting you ready to fight for your life or to run for your life. That is what stress really is. Your mind thinks about something that worries or upsets you, and your body feels stress. Faster than you can even talk about it, your body is ready to fight or to run, but your mind is no longer able to do anything very well.

And so you set yourself up to fail. The truth is that when you cannot think very clearly, you cannot do well. You fail tests. You say the wrong thing to a boy or girl you like. If you can't think well, you fail.

12 | *Another Problem*

Besides making it hard to think well, those same hormones in your blood can also make you quite sick. Often, they can keep your sickness defense from working. The germs that can make you sick are usually killed by your sickness defense, called your immune system.

But stress keeps your immune system from fighting the germs. So you get sick.

Think about it. Remember the last time you had a cold or the flu? Was something stressful going on in your life at that time? It's quite likely that you got the cold just before or during or after something that stressed you. You worry about something, the hormones stay in your blood for a while, and you get sick.

The Good Part

But stress can sometimes also help you. If you are facing a deadline to turn in a paper, the hormones can help you adapt to the extra demand on you. Many people say they work best when on a deadline. Many athletes turn in their best performances when facing stiff competition. The so-called fight-or-flight reaction gives the quarterback the extra burst of energy to score the winning touchdown.

Athletes like Carl Lewis work with stress to help them win in competition.

14   So the trick in managing your stress is
understanding what is going on in your
body. If you feel under stress, ask yourself
a few questions: What is the worst thing
that can happen? (Probably nothing very
bad!) Have I done everything I can to
make the situation come out right? Will I
remember it a few years from now?

People who do not understand stress
and who let themselves give in to it may be
tempted to try dangerous ways to get rid
of it. They may make everything worse by
turning to drugs.

CHAPTER 2

Taking Drugs: A Good Idea or Not?

*L*en Bias was the greatest basketball player in the history of the University of Maryland. He was smart. He was a true leader. He was a good student. He was an All-American.

When Len finished his college career, he was drafted by the Boston Celtics, a professional basketball team. The Celtics flew Len Bias to Boston. He was on TV and in all the newspapers. His family and friends were so proud of him.

Len signed a contract to play for the Celtics. The money from the contract would make him a millionaire. And he was barely twenty years old!

16 Len flew back to the University of
Maryland. That night he was with several
of his best friends. They were happy for
him, and they all talked about the future
and how it would be.

They decided to use some drugs. Why?
Weren't they happy enough without taking
something to make them "feel different"?
No one knows. We only know that Len
used cocaine. And we know that in just a
few seconds the cocaine killed Len Bias.

So Len never got to see his wonderful
future. He just died there in his college
dorm room. His name was known by
almost every person in America who read
the sports pages. Now Len is just a
memory.

Getting Messed Up

Not every person who uses drugs dies.
Some do die. Others just get messed up.
Sports stars, movie stars, singing stars,
other famous people—and thousands of
people whose names you never heard—get
messed up from drugs every year. What
does "messed up" mean? It means that
their lives stop working, and if they are
lucky, they go someplace where people can
help them to "be human" again. It means
that they begin to "need" their drugs, and

Drugs may lead to loss of control over your life.

18 that without the drugs they are not able to feel "right." It can mean that they become addicted to a drug—they need more and more of it or else they feel awful all the time.

An addict must have more and more of a drug and feels worse and worse without it. The drug becomes the only thing in life that matters. People can be addicted to drugs and alcohol. Becoming an addict can really mess up your life—maybe forever.

Courtney Love

Courtney Love is a rock star and an actress. She is also a widow and a single mother. Her husband, Kurt Cobain, the lead singer of Nirvana, had trouble dealing with the pressures of fame, and became addicted to heroin. Some believe this led him to commit suicide, leaving behind Courtney and their daughter, Frances Bean.

Courtney also used drugs, and there were reports that she had used heroin before and after her pregnancy. On several occasions, Courtney has been harmed by drugs. The bass player for her band, Kristin Pfaff, overdosed on heroin. Courtney, herself, has had to go to hospitals

and rehabilitation centers to get off drugs.
She has accidentally overdosed and has
tried to commit suicide, too.

Some people look at famous rock stars
who do drugs and think, "They're rich and
famous. They get to play music. How have
drugs hurt them?" Courtney Love knows.
She has lost friends, fans, and most impor-
tantly, her husband, all because of drugs.

Courtney could have kept using, but she
realized that there are things in life, like
her daughter, more important than drugs.
Now, Courtney is off drugs and is getting
acclaim as an actress. She was nominated
for a Golden Globe award for *The People
vs. Larry Flynt* in 1996, and is teaching
her daughter to stay away from drugs.

Peer Pressure

No one will ever know exactly why Len
Bias used cocaine. Some people said it was
the first time he had ever tried it. Was it because his friend urged him to do it?

That kind of urging by friends is called
peer pressure. Such pressure can be very
stressful even if it does not concern drugs.

Part of a teen's life is the pressure to be
like everyone else. Another part is wanting
to be liked, to fit in, to be a part of

Teens who don't smoke, drink, or do drugs have to resist peer pressure.

22 | the gang. Peer pressure can lead you in good directions or bad. It can make you work harder to get the same good grades that your clique considers cool. Or it can make you listen to a friend who suggests shoplifting lipstick at the cosmetics counter or an all-purpose Swiss Army knife in the sports department.

Good or bad, peer pressure is strong among teenagers. And it can be stressful. Healthy stress helps you get the A grade. And negative stress can come from listening to your friend who thought stealing was okay.

Teen Drug Use

While teens are less likely to use drugs now than in the last fifteen years, surveys released in 1996 indicate a huge increase of drug use among teens from 1992 to 1995. It seems that many teens are using drugs to help relieve their stress. One survey from the Substance Abuse and Mental Health Services Administration said that drugs were used by 10.9 percent of those between ages twelve and seventeen in 1995. Compare that to 8.2 percent in 1994 and only 5.3 percent in 1992. The survey also included the following:

 • Marijuana use increased 141 percent.

- Cocaine use increased 166 percent.   **23**
- LSD and other hallucinogen use
  increased 183 percent.

Another survey, called the Monitoring
the Future survey from the University of
Michigan, reported that drug use has
increased because more younger kids are
starting to use drugs. In fact, drug use
among high school seniors has appeared to
level off. That survey shows:

- The amount of 8th-graders who used
  marijuana in the past month increased
  from 3 percent to 11 percent. Among
  10th-graders, use rose from 9 percent to
  20 percent.
- The amount of 8th-graders who said
  they drink alcohol everyday doubled
  from 0.5 percent to 1 percent.

Drug use by teens has gotten worse
every year since 1991. Cigarette use has
also increased. In a recent survey, one-fifth
of 8th-graders said they smoked a cigarette
within the last month. More than one-third
of high school seniors also smoke cigarettes.

In 1995 *The Columbia University College
of Physicians & Surgeons Complete Home
Medical Guide* stated that almost two-thirds
of American teenagers experiment with
drugs before they finish high school. They
quoted a survey that said 7 percent used

Coffee, alcohol, cigarettes, and other everyday drugs all have an effect on the body's systems.

marijuana daily, 6 percent drank alcohol daily, and 20 percent smoked cigarettes daily. It's hard to say which drug is the most dangerous. Some reports rank alcohol as the most harmful drug. The report also listed the most common pattern of drug use:

1. Beer and wine are the first drugs used by teens.
2. Tobacco and hard liquor are next.
3. Marijuana is tried next, often with alcohol.
4. Illicit drugs like LSD, cocaine, or heroin may be used next.

Do you know people who follow this pattern? Has drug use increased with the people you know at your school?

It's hard to say whether the increase in drug use is due to stress, peer pressure, or the changing times. Maybe it is a combination of all three. Drugs won't make life better. Why add more stress to your life?

In Search of the Good Life

Do you have a good life right now? Do you hope to have one in the future? Here is a list of the Top Ten Worries among teenagers. The list outlines the many concerns teenagers have about the future.

1. Having a good marriage and family life
2. Choosing the right job or finding steady work
3. Doing well in school
4. Doing well in a job or line of work
5. Having good friends
6. Paying for college
7. America "going downhill"
8. Making a lot of money
9. Finding goals and meaning in life
10. Getting AIDS

These are the things teenagers worry about the most. What drugs will help you deal with your top ten worries?

None of the illegal drugs can help. They can only keep you from having a good family life, choosing the right job, doing well in school, being successful, having friends, or almost anything else that would be good in life.

What about legal drugs? We see (on TV, at least) people with good jobs, nice clothes, and money, who drink alcohol, smoke cigarettes, and drink beverages with caffeine. So, is there a problem with those drugs? Yes. Alcohol is the cause of 40,000 deaths a year and cigarettes is the main cause of lung cancer, heart attacks, and other deaths.

What's the Problem?

Any drug—even caffeine and nicotine— can be a problem if you use it all the time. You begin to "need" it in your mind, and maybe in your body. You are no longer in control of yourself. *Being out of control is the most stressful way to be.* You are stressed when you do not have control of what happens to you.

No one plans to be an addict. It just happens. It happens a lot faster than you might think. By the time you realize that you are hooked on a drug, it is too late to easily stop. Stopping takes time and effort and, usually, help from other people. And it will be stressful.

It's weird, isn't it? People take drugs because they feel stressed. Taking drugs soon makes them more stressed than they were before. And then stopping the drugs is even more stressful for a while. It would make a lot more sense to learn to handle stress *without* drugs, wouldn't it?

Ann's Story

In Northern Virginia, a girl named Ann told her story to *The Washington Post.* Ann was an alcoholic and drug addict by the time she was fifteen years old. Her life had

28 | become so stressful that she thought drugs were the only answer. But drinking and using drugs just added to the stress, and trying to stop taking drugs was the most stressful part of all.

When Ann was thirteen, her older sister gave Ann her first beer. Two years later, she was drinking all the time to help her deal with the pain of her daily life. Her parents had gotten divorced when she was in the fifth grade, and she was living with her mother and stepfather in Nebraska. By the time she entered junior high, her stepfather was yelling at her all the time. "He would totally cut me down," she said.

So Ann moved in with her father and stepmother in Northern Virginia. Even though she was starting over in a new school in a different environment, Ann received good grades and even made the cheerleading squad. She got along with her father and stepmother, too, but that didn't last long. Soon, Ann and her stepmother were fighting. Her father and stepmother were fighting too. Eventually, Ann and her father moved into a place of their own. Ann's father decided that Ann should go to a military academy.

Ann's father knew that Ann was drinking and that there were kids who did drugs at

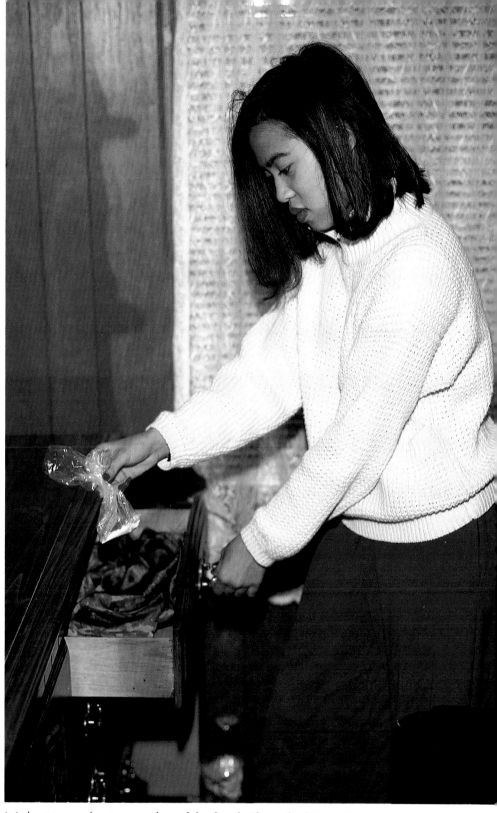

It is best to confront a member of the family if you find drugs in your home.

30 | her old school. He wanted to get her away from the bad influences. Soon after Ann got to the military academy she called her father. "All the kids here are doing drugs," she said. "I want to come home." Ann's father didn't bring her home. Shortly thereafter, Ann smoked her first marijuana cigarette with her boyfriend.

Ann said her boyfriend didn't pressure her to smoke marijuana. Peer pressure isn't always the way adults think it is, she says. You want to copy what other people do. But nobody actually says, "Do this or you're not cool." "You're thinking, 'Gosh, if all these people are doing it, it must not be so bad,'" Ann said.

Ann started smoking marijuana a lot after that. She was suspended from the academy after they found drugs in her room. Her father brought her home and enrolled her in public school. This would bring Ann to the lowest point of her life.

One night Ann's father came home with some beer and got drunk with her. She was fifteen years old. Ann's father was an alcoholic. He decided to get Ann drunk so she wouldn't tell anybody that he was drinking again. Ann threw up four times that night, but her father was too drunk to do anything to help.

Possession of drugs may lead to arrest.

Saying no to drugs is the best way to prevent addiction.

Ann realized that she needed to get help. She joined a 12-step program, a program where recovering alcoholics, called sponsors, help each other stop drinking. In the program, Ann learned that alcoholism was a lifelong disease that she would have to deal with. That night with her father was the last night she drank alcohol.

But she continued to smoke marijuana. This led Ann to miss more than thirty days of school one winter. Her father kept drinking and sometimes locked her out of the house. One time, she ran away for two days. When she returned she told her dad that she'd been raped. He took her to the hospital, and then checked himself into a program to stop drinking.

Ann was sent to live with the man who was sponsoring her father in his 12-step program. However, the man's son, a high school senior, was a drug dealer, and kept giving Ann marijuana. Ann knew she couldn't stay there. After a month, Ann told the boy's parents their son was dealing drugs and that she had to leave.

Ann moved back with her father and vowed to stay off drugs. But on her sixteenth birthday, she smoked marijuana again. The next day, Ann called her mother to see if she could visit her in Nebraska. Ann's mother said no. She didn't trust Ann not to do drugs. Ann was hurt and swore she would never talk to her mother again.

When her father returned home that night, Ann threatened to kill herself if he didn't start spending more time with her. He took Ann to the hospital to find a treatment center where he could take Ann to get her off of drugs.

When Ann first started the program, she didn't make much progress. But after a while, she realized she could talk to the counselors and that they could help her. Finally, Ann had someone she could talk

34   to about her problems with her parents, with school, and with drugs. When she completed her time at the center, she was voted the most improved patient.

Ann has had a lot of problems, but she's lucky. She was never arrested. She never got pregnant. She never had any severe physical side effects. And she's still alive. Still, her life would have been a lot better if she'd never gotten involved in drugs in the first place.

Staying Away from Drugs

We've talked about stress. We've talked about how people use drugs because they are stressed. We've talked about how using drugs makes people much more stressed than they were before. You've learned about how trying to stop using drugs is the most stressful thing of all. And you have read a true story about how drugs can affect your life.

Drugs are not the answer to any problem. They will make your problems worse, and possibly ruin your life.

Stress can mess you up. Stress can make you fail. Stress can make you sick. But you *can* handle stress without drugs. And that makes a lot more sense.

CHAPTER 3

Making Your Life Good

A famous teacher once studied dogs. Dogs act like people sometimes. We know right away when a dog is happy, or scared, or mad, or confused.

The teacher studied dogs who were kept in a small room (in his lab) with no doors or windows. At first the dogs tried to get out. When they learned that there was no way out, they gave up. They just sat there.

When the teacher put the dogs in a small room with a window, they still just sat there. They had learned that you can't get out of a small room, so they didn't try.

Finally the teacher put the dogs in a small room with an open door. An open door! And still the dogs just sat there. They had learned that you can't get out of a small room, so they didn't try.

36   The teacher noticed that people are the same way. When people find out that they can't do something, they stop trying. They often stop trying to do anything at all just because they can't do one thing.

How about you? Have you stopped trying to do everything just because you can't yet do one thing? It is easy to begin to feel that you can't make it.

In Chapter 2 we talked about the fact that being out of control is the most stressful way to be. That is why school is stressful. You are not in control of what happens to you there. In school you may find that reading is hard, and so you may feel that everything is hard—too hard.

That is what the teacher meant when he said that dogs *and* people stop trying when they find they can't do something. They stop trying to do anything at all.

Being in control means feeling that you can learn to do anything you really want to do. When you learn to have that feeling, nothing is too stressful. You are sure that you can handle anything that comes your way. Remember our list of the 10 Top Worries among teenagers. Included in the list were marriage and jobs and school and friends and college and money.

Drug-free teens enjoy life and have positive attitudes.

38   Do you feel in control when you think of things like that? Do you feel that you know how to get those things? Or have you stopped trying?

Walter Anderson

One person who got control of his life is a man named Walter Anderson. As a child, Walter lived in an abusive home and his family didn't have much money. Walter's school was in a nice part of town, so he had to go to school with people who were more wealthy than he was. Sometimes this hurt Walter's confidence.

When he was sixteen, Walter decided to quit high school and join the Marine Corps. The Marines told him to come back when he was seventeen. A week after his seventeenth birthday, Walter enlisted.

Part of the physical fitness training in the Marine Corps is to successfully complete the obstacle course, or "confidence course." According to Walter, "the function [of the course] is to build confidence, not to present obstacles. Obstacles exist for you to gain confidence." When Walter joined the Marine Corps, he overcame the obstacle of living in an abusive environment and gained confidence.

Being involved in positive activities creates joy and satisfaction.

After leaving the Marines, Walter went to college where he was a summa cum laude graduate with a degree in psychology. He then worked for various newspapers and became an editor. After that, he was hired by *Parade Magazine* and became its senior editor. Since then, *Parade Magazine*'s circulation has risen to more than 37 million with over 80 million

40 readers, making it the most widely read magazine in the country.

Since Walter knows first hand how hard it is to grow up without a support system, he is involved with programs designed to help people who need it. He is on the boards of the Literacy Volunteers of America, the National Center for Family Literacy, and he's the national spokesperson for the GED program, which helps high school dropouts get their equivalency diplomas. He is also the director of the National Dropout Prevention Fund. In 1996 he was appointed to the U.S. National Commission on Libraries and Information Science by President Bill Clinton.

Walter also writes self-help books. His fourth book is called *The Confidence Course*. Modeled after the physical obstacle courses of the Marines, this book helps people who lack self-esteem find solutions to problems in their lives. Walter also teaches a college course called "The Confidence Course."

In his book, Walter talks about the "Seven Steps to Fulfillment." 1. Know who is responsible (you). 2. Believe in something big. 3. Practice tolerance. 4. Be brave. 5. Love someone. 6. Be ambitious. 7. Smile.

These steps are pretty simple. And the first one is probably the most important.

It takes steady, hard work to reach the goals you set in life.

42 You are the one who's responsible for your life. It's easier to blame somebody when things go wrong, but in the end, each of us is responsible for our own happiness.

Not everyone can join the Marines like Walter did, but his example is clear. He took responsibility for himself. Instead of turning to drugs or crime, he went for something that gave him confidence. He believed in himself enough to take control of his life. Do you?

Hopes and Goals

You need three hooks on which to hang your hopes for making your life good:

- You need goals for yourself.
- You need a high school diploma.
- You need an adult you can trust.

What should your goals be? Think about the list of worries. There is one thing that affects nearly every item on the list—your education.

If you are in high school right now, you can graduate from high school. If you want, you can also graduate from a two-year or a four-year college. And you can make your whole life as good as you want it to be.

A few years ago a group of teachers studied people who had made good lives. What do you think those people had in common?

The main thing was that they all got a college degree, which means that they also got a high school diploma. It did not matter how much money their families had or did not have. It did not matter how good their grades were in high school, as long as they were able to graduate. It did not matter what college they attended. It did not matter whether or not they had to borrow money to go to college.

It just mattered that they went, and they finished.

How can you do that? How can you graduate from high school, go to a two-year or a four-year college, and graduate from that school, too?

You can learn to read as well as you can. You can learn to handle the stress of it all, so that you can do well in tests and not get sick while you are working toward this goal. You can learn that you must stay in control of you. That means that you must know that drugs cannot help you and will almost surely keep you from your goal.

Remember, the first two "Hooks for Your Hopes" are setting solid goals and

44 graduating from school. We have just agreed that these two "hooks" are really parts of one thing: your education. If your education is your main goal, you have two of your three "Hooks for Your Hopes."

What about that third "hook"—an adult you can trust? Why is that important? It is important because any student, no matter how smart, needs to be able to talk to someone who has gone through high school and college and can help.

With a pencil and paper, make a list of numbers 1 through 17. Go through the list of "Adults You Can Trust." Make a check mark beside any adult who is a good listener or friendly or available to you.

Really think about this. It is important. You will do much better with your first two "Hooks for Your Hopes" if you also have this third "hook."

Did any adults on your list have three check marks? Were there any with two? Those adults are the ones to whom you should seriously consider talking.

If no adults on your list have two or three check marks, you need to choose one of your teachers or coaches or counselors or principals and explain that you need an adult you can trust.

Adults You Can Trust

Good Listener   Friendly   Available

1. Mother or stepmother or foster mother   _____

2. Father or stepfather or foster father   _____

3. Adult sister or brother   _____

4. Aunt or uncle   _____

5. Grandmother or grandfather   _____

6. Adult relative other than the above   _____

7. A teacher   _____

8. A counselor   _____

9. A principal   _____

10. A coach   _____

11. A music director (or other director of special activities)   _____

12. A minister, priest, or rabbi   _____

13. A neighbor   _____

14. An adult "boss" at your summer or after-school job   _____

15. An admissions counselor at any college of interest to you   _____

16. Other professional "helpers"   _____

17. Any other adults (list by name):   _____

Finding someone to talk to can be the first step in recovering from a drug problem.

If that sounds too hard, *just ask him or her to read this book*. That will make it clear. In fact, that is the best way to make it clear to any adult.

What will the trusted adult do for you? First of all, he or she will listen to you. And you must talk. You must tell this person why you have decided that your education is important to you now.

Say that you want to stay in control of your life. Say that you want to make your life good, that you want to be able to handle the stress of life, and that you want no part of drugs.

Your trusted adult can probably take it from there. He or she can help you look at the courses you are taking in high school. He or she can help you learn how to take tests better. He or she can help you get help with your reading skills. He or she can help you think about college. He or she can help you get information on how to get in and how to get help with the money problems that all students have when they go to college.

Your trusted adult can be of great help to you in meeting your goals. Choose one. Take this book with you. Talk to him or her. *It will be worth the effort*.

Daily physical exercise can be helpful in relieving stress.

CHAPTER 4

Winning

We have talked about drugs. We have talked about stress and about being in control. We have talked about goals. We have talked about your education and about your trusted adult.

Now it is time to think harder about stress control. We have seen what stress can do: It makes you fail; it makes you sick. We have seen that using drugs just makes stress worse. We have seen that using drugs means that you will fail for sure, and in worse ways. We have seen that learning to handle stress puts you in control.

This chapter is called "Winning" because if you learn stress control, you

50 can win in anything. How? By winning over yourself. Stress will defeat you if you let it. Stress control allows you to defeat stress and to be at your best.

Do you play basketball? Do you watch other people play basketball? Think about the last time you shot a free throw or saw someone else shoot a free throw. What happened just before you made the shot after the referee gave you the ball?

Probably you or the player you watched took hold of the ball. You took one or two very deep breaths, relaxed the hand and arm you were going to shoot with, and *then* you shot.

Did the shot go in? Maybe. It doesn't really matter. But somehow you knew that it was more likely to go in if you first took deep breaths and relaxed your arm. So the first thing you did was to defeat your stress. Then you shot.

That was stress control.

Without it, you were likely to miss your shot. With it, you were more likely to make it.

The same is true in your classes and in anything else you do. With stress control, you are more likely to do well. Without stress control, you are less likely to do well.

All achievers deal with and manage stress on a daily basis. Here, the winners of the 42nd annual Westinghouse Science Talent Search, celebrate their achievements.

52   Remember in Chapter 1 we talked about upsetting thoughts that cause your body to make hormones. Those little drops in your blood make you feel tense and uptight. They make butterflies in your stomach. They make it very hard to *think* clearly.

How could a deep breath and a relaxed body do anything to help you? Normal breathing and a relaxed body keep your mind and body from getting more upset. Normal breathing and a relaxed body make your mind and body think that you are in control. You feel that you do not need more stress hormones in your blood. And so you have *controlled your stress*. You have done stress control. It is that simple.

How can you remember to do stress control when you are having worried or upsetting thoughts? One good way is called Counting Down.

To use Counting Down, think of your body as having three parts. Part Three is your face. Part Two is your body. Part One is your legs.

When you feel yourself starting to get worried, no matter where you are or what you are doing, say to yourself quickly, "Three, Two, One."

As you say "Three," relax your facial muscles (especially your jaw).

As you say "Two," take a very long, slow breath.

As you say "One," relax your legs.

That's it. That is one of the very best ways to do stress control. It takes only a couple of seconds. No one else knows you are doing it. You can do it a hundred times a day. It's easy. *And it works.*

It is *your* Counting Down and *your* stress control. And so it puts you back in control anytime *you* choose.

Drugs are of no use in making your life good. Stress control is. Being in control is. Having solid goals is. Getting your education is. Having a trusted adult is.

That is what winning really means. It means defeating stress and all the other things that can get in the way of making your life good. You can start winning. Just decide.

CHAPTER 5

Your Contract

*A*nytime you decide to change yourself, or to set goals, or to make your life better, you need to write it down. Everybody does.

We all do better that way. We see on paper what we have decided to do. We see on paper what steps we must take. And so we do better. We know what to do. And we know when we have done it.

A contract is just that. It is a promise to yourself, written on paper.

Following is a sample contract. Look at it carefully. Then make one for yourself. You don't need to show it to anyone except your trusted adult. You will want that person to see it so you can talk about it and think about it. That person can help

you make your contract happen.

A Sample Contract

For the three-month period starting —————————
and ending ————————— .

My Goals—
I. Education
    A. Homework: Each night before I go to sleep I
       will work on my *hardest* subject for 45
       minutes (even if I could do it in less time).

    B. Homework: Each night before I go to sleep, I
       will read aloud from one of my school books
       for 30 minutes.

    C. Teachers: I will meet with every teacher I
       have to tell them that I want to do well and
       to give them a chance to tell me how I might
       improve. I will do this once every four weeks.

II. Drugs and Stress
    A. Every night I will pretend to be taking a test
       or talking to a teacher or something else
       stressful, and I will do Counting Down for
       practice.

    B. Every night I will think about how I can
       make sure that tomorrow will be drug-free
       for me—no contact with people who sell or
       use drugs, and no actions of any kind that
       will keep me from being in control of my
       own life.

Writing down your goals helps to keep you on track.

For your contract to work, you need to write it yourself. It can be as short as you want to make it, or as long. But you must remember, to succeed with goals, there should only be a few. Work on just a few things at a time. Get good at each goal. Then you can write a new one.

Look at your contract every single day to make sure you are doing what you have said you would. Talk to your trusted adult about it at least once a week. You must let that person help you. All of us do better if we can talk with someone we trust about our goals every day or every week.

This is all you need to start to make your life better and to be in control of what happens to you. Share this book with others who need to get control of their own lives. Talk with them about it. Get your friends to care about being in control of their lives. Help them. And help yourself.

You can do this.

Where to Go for Help

American Council for Drug Education
164 West 74th Street
New York, NY 10023
(212) 758-8060
(800) 488-DRUG

Center for Substance Abuse Treatment Information and Treatment Referral Hot Line
11426-28 Rockville Pike
Rockville, MD 20852
(800) 622-HELP

Families Anonymous, Inc.
P.O. Box 3475
Culver City, CA 90231
(310) 313-5800
(800) 736-9805

Nar-Anon Family Groups
P.O. Box 2562
Palos Verdes Peninsula, CA 90274
(310) 547-5800

Narcotics Anonymous (NA)
P.O. Box 9999
Van Nuys, CA 91409
(818) 773-9999

National Clearinghouse for Alcohol and Drug Information
P.O. Box 2345
Rockville, MD 20847
(301) 468-2600
(800) 729-6686

National Council on Alcoholic and Drug Dependence
12 West 21st Street
New York, NY 10010
(800) 622-2255

National Families in Action
2296 Henderson Mill Road
Atlanta, GA 30345
(404) 934-6364

Glossary
Explaining New Words

AA (Alcoholics Anonymous) Group of people who are addicted to alcohol and who meet often to help one another stay away from drinking.

addiction Need for more and more of a drug in order to feel "normal."

AIDS (acquired immune deficiency syndrome) Fatal disease caused by the human immunodeficiency virus (HIV). It is transmitted through blood and other body fluids, especially during sexual activity or intravenous drug use.

contract An agreement between people to do, or not to do, some action.

60 **drug** Chemical substance that changes the functioning of the body. It may be used in the treatment of an illness or to alter the state of one's mind, as in illegal drugs.

goal An aim or a purpose toward which one works and which one hopes to achieve.

hormones Chemical substances that flow through your bloodstream and affect the activity of body organs.

immune system Body system that fights disease.

stress Pressure caused by the body's physical or emotional response to outside events.

For Further Reading

Ardel, Don, and Tager, Mark. *Planning for Wellness*. Dubuque, IA: Kendall/Hunt, 1982.

Ball, Jacqueline. *Everything You Need to Know About Drug Abuse*, rev. ed. New York: Rosen Publishing Group, 1992.

Berger, Gilda. *Meg's Story. Get Real: Straight Talk About Drugs*. Brookfield, CT: Millbrook Press, 1992.

Gooden, Kimberly Wood. *Coping with Family Stress*. New York: Rosen Publishing Group, 1989.

Keyishian, Elizabeth. *Everything You Need to Know About Smoking*, rev. ed. New York: Rosen Publishing Group, 1993.

62 Lanbone, John. *Tough Choices: A Book About Substance Abuse.* Boston: Little Brown & Co., 1995.

McFarland, Rhoda. *Coping with Substance Abuse*, rev. ed. New York: Rosen Publishing Group, 1990.

Sehnert, Keith. *Stress/Unstress.* Minneapolis, MN: Augsburg, 1981.

Washburne, Carolyn Kott. *Drug Abuse.* San Diego: Lucent Books, Inc., 1996.

Index

63

About the Author

Dr. M. Walker Buckalew researches human stress and has taught courses in stress control for the Education Department of St. Lawrence University, Canton, New York. Prior to that, Dr. Buckalew spent six years teaching English and coaching a variety of sports. He is the author of several books on stress.

Photo Credits

Cover photo by Stuart Rabinowitz. Pages 13, 51 © AP/ Wide World Photos; page 31 © Roger M. Richards/Gamma-Liaison; all other photos by Stuart Rabinowitz.